T0194983

TELLING HER STORY

Inspired by His Love, Mercy, and Grace

ENLIGHTENED

WESTBOW
PRESS®
A DIVISION OF THOMAS NELSON
& ZONDERVAN

WestBow Press books may be ordered through booksellers or by contacting:

WestBow Press
A Division of Thomas Nelson & Zondervan
1663 Liberty Drive
Bloomington, IN 47403
www.westbowpress.com
1 (866) 928-1240

All Scripture quotations are taken from The Holy Bible, New
International Version®, NIV® Copyright © 1973, 1978, 1984, 2011 by
Biblica, Inc.® Used by permission. All rights reserved worldwide.

ISBN: 978-1-9736-9148-8 (sc)
ISBN: 978-1-9736-9149-5 (hc)
ISBN: 978-1-9736-9147-1 (e)

Library of Congress Control Number: 2020908828

Print information available on the last page.

WestBow Press rev. date: 5/26/2020

CONTENTS

INTRODUCTION VII

CHAPTER ONE 1

CHAPTER TWO 5

CHAPTER THREE 17

CHAPTER FOUR 27

CHAPTER FIVE 49
Marriage

CHAPTER SIX 61
Sister's New Location

CHAPTER SEVEN 67
Repented Life

CHAPTER EIGHT 71

CHAPTER NINE 93
Loving God the Father, Son, and Holy Spirit

ABOUT THE AUTHOR 103

INTRODUCTION

Who are You?

What is your response when asked this question?

Is your response based on your opinion or the opinion determined by others?

Have the opinions, standards, acceptance and rejection of others formed you into who you are?

Have you considered identifying who you are without including the opinions of others?

Do you love yourself?

This is a nonfiction story of someone who is sharing her story to help others identify who they are from a different perspective. We live in a world that has so many complex issues. It is difficult to navigate as there are so many people and factors who are involved both directly and indirectly. Many people are misunderstood as others really do not know "your story."

It is believed that the story begins before one's time of conception and birth. Everyone seems to desire to be loved. Although not knowing exactly what love is, there is yet a desire or yearning for what love provides. The infant desires it from the parent(s) as he or she cries out for the things that are attributes of love. It's things such as attention, a tender embrace, and other fulfillments of one's need.

The children desire love from the parent(s) or guardian during their upbringing. The adults desire it from others as they engage in relationships and/or marriage. The love relationships are not without issues. These issues affect the lives of some individuals more drastically than others.

Sister is allowing her life and love experiences to be shared by having her story told. She desires to help anyone who is searching for a relationship full of love. It is a love that is beyond anything less than being miraculous. Once you engage in this love relationship, you will never be the same. The success of receiving it is that you always remember, reflect, and apply it in the form of an everlasting love relationship with the only One who can provide it for you. After you receive it, mature through it, you in turn, will extend the agape love to others.

Telling Her Story is about "Sister" who goes down many paths during her life experiences and it isn't until she takes the Word of God as her navigator, does she come to surrender to His directions to the path He wants her to travel.

A nonfiction testimony of the life of a Christian child, mother, woman, grandmother, and Ordained Minister. Life is a journey and there are many paths. While missing many signs and turning in the wrong directions she finally realized she needed a road map. Not knowing how to navigate it she continued to go down into the valleys and was lost. She finally realized she had to learn how to read the map (Bible) so she prayed and asked God to show her. He gave her the Special map (Bible) that also referenced the path of His Son Jesus Christ. God also provided her with His Holy Spirit to lead her through not only through the path of the world but a path all the more leading to the eternal relationship with Him.

CHAPTER ONE

About three years ago, she, who I will refer to as "Sister," was spiritually inspired to write a book. It was during a period of her being overwhelmed by many trials and tribulations. Sister had no understanding of why her life was in turmoil. It was not a period of days, weeks, or months; they were years of pain and agony in many facets of her life.

As the thought to write a book came to mind, she initially rejected it because she did not believe God was telling her to expose her life story. On the other hand, she remembered a conversation that she had with her mother when she told her, "I want to write a book about my life, and I want to include something you know I had to keep secret during most of my life."

Her mother, knowing exactly what she was implying, asked Sister to wait until after her death because she did not want anyone to judge her. Her mother said, "I know that I will have to answer to God for this after I die." Although painful to hear, Sister did respect her wishes and approval. So, she did not begin to write until after her mother's passing.

As she was writing the draft of the book, she wondered if it was truly God inspiring her to write or was it that she needed to unload her suitcases of burdens. She concluded that if it was of God, He would direct the path to it being published. Once the draft was complete, she stepped out in faith as she went on the internet and reached out to various authors and publishers. There was one publishing company she thought might publish the book. After sending in the manuscript, they notified her it was approved for consideration.

She was so excited, but it was short-lived. Within days of receiving the acceptance, she received an unexpected phone call from the publishing company. There was an additional requirement in order to proceed. A down payment was needed. Sister thought that with it being approved, the publishing company would provide the author with the option of having the costs deducted from the book's profit. But this was not so. Although painful to hear and understand the terms, payment was required to proceed. Sister, not having the required fees, researched other approaches to having the book published, but her efforts were unsuccessful.

She wondered if it was not God's will for her to write the book. She really did not know the answer, but she certainly felt better after releasing all that baggage in her writing. Throughout this endeavor, Sister sent a backup copy of the chapters to her cousin. This cousin was like a beloved mother, sister, and friend all in one person. She told Sister, "I believe that God did want you to submit the book, but He wants you to experience some other things to include in it as you are still growing in the Lord." The cousin believed that after the period of more tests, trials, and developments, Sister would be ready to resubmit her book for publication. I agree with the cousin, and I believe the time has come.

Sister was so thankful for her encouraging words. They both believed and had faith in the Sovereign God, who has a divine purpose and plan for everyone's life. After completing the manuscript, Sister expected God to perform more miracles in her life. Sister believed she would be delivered out of experiences she had encountered and had an inspired spiritual contrast with what is written in the Bible regarding Daniel being thrown into the lion's den (Daniel 6:16), or Shadrach, Meshach, and Abednego thrown into the blazing furnace (Daniel 3:22, 23).

To Sister, it seemed like she left a lion's den and went straight into the fiery furnace. As soon as she entered, it was as if someone turned up the furnace and broke the off switch. Things escalated for the worse. It was yet another season of chaos, pain, suffering, embarrassment, humiliation, devastation, and other various forms of agony.

There is so much more to speak about her life than what is written in this book, but I want to tell her story from the standpoint of segments of her secular and Christian lives and journeys.

CHAPTER TWO

Sister was about five years old and for whatever reason, remembered her life from that time forward. The first day of remembrance was her father taking her to school. A few children in the class said and did mean things to her, and they hit her. Students are still subjected to such bullying by other children at various times in their education. The difference is that when Sister was a victim, it was not referred to as bullying. Rather, it was considered part of normal childlike behavior. In the time since Sister was in school, the development of modern technology has allowed for recording these assaults and shown on the news and the internet. The criminal justice system also prosecutes various forms of attack. Bullying is no longer restricted to specific geographical areas, communities, races, religious beliefs, or ages. And verbal and physical assaults are increasing at a significant rate.

Sister grew up in a community of mixed population. There were African Americans, Caucasians, Italians, Irish, Polish, and so on. The people were nice. Children were required to respect their neighbors and adults.

When Sister was about six or seven, her mother had her to go to the local grocery store almost every other day. It was only around the corner. Her mother, born in the South, had an eighth-grade education because as an adolescent she was required to work in the field instead of going to school. Sister therefore had to write down the grocery list. Sister was the one who initially asked the store owner if they could have food on credit. There were two stores that she went to during the week. If the bill at one store got too high and her parents could not pay it that week, she went to the other store. At times it was embarrassing for her because the store owner would say, "No, you can't get anything because you haven't paid the bill!" Her parents did not have to hear this as they never went to the local store.

Neighbors sitting on their porches would, of course, see her going to the store. Most times they asked her to get something for them. One neighbor, who was in a wheelchair, would yell out from across the street, "Come here, girl." Sister would go over to him, and he would tell her what he wanted from the store. She would have to reach into his top shirt pocket to get the money because he could not use one hand and arm. It was believed he had a stroke that limited his mobility.

Another neighbor frequently wanted a newspaper. She had to go to another store down the street to get it because they did not sell it at the other two stores.

Next door to her house was an older man in a wheelchair lived with his adult daughter. When she went to work, she left the main door of the two-family home unlocked so Sister could go and find out what he wanted from the local store and then bring in the groceries when she returned. As an African American child and this neighbor being a Caucasian, you might think that the family would have reservations, but this was the kind of community she grew up in. They loved and respected each other.

Since Sister's parents did not have a telephone at that time, this elderly, handicapped neighbor would let her know when he wanted something from the

From time to time, her mother attended a Holiness church. She only went a few times, but Sister went more often as she mainly was the only other one from the family transported to the church. The female pastor resided in the community, and her husband took some attendees in his station wagon. At the church, the women wore long dresses and skirts. Sister liked going there but went to the Presbyterian church more often.

Sister's family lacked many things financially, but her mother made sure they did not lack attendance at a church. Lack of attendance at school was another issue. Sister was so disappointed when she could not attend school the first week because her parents could not afford to buy new school clothes for her and her siblings. One time, after a few days of the new school session, her mother bought her a couple of dresses, but she could not afford new shoes. Her mother took a pair of old shoes, polished them, and placed a piece of cardboard inside them to cover the hole in the bottom of the shoe. Sister had a friend in the sixth grade who exchanged shoes with Sister. On their walk to school, she loaned Sister her new shoes and wore Sister's old pair. At the end of the school day they would exchange shoes before they returned home. Their parents never knew.

There were other times during elementary school that Sister missed many days because her brother was ill. Both her parents worked, and since she was the only daughter for a period, she was the chosen one to babysit. Surely, they were not going to deny the boys, as the two older siblings, to miss school. Her ill brother, who was the youngest, had broken his hip. For a few months, he was in a cast from his hip to his kneecap and unable to get up. There was a bar extended and attached from one cast leg to the other. The only opening was in his private and rectal area so he could use the bedpan. Yes, she had to be attentive to that as well as bathing him and preparing his meals.

When Sister was able to go to school, there were times when there was a lot of makeup homework from missing so many days. She was able to complete it without the help of the parents. Her mother could not assist because of her educational limitations, and the father worked and did not offer to help. He was an educated, veteran and worked at that time in a factory. He mandated that the interior of his house be clean. He had better not come home to a dirty house or dishes in the sink. Sister's brothers sometimes intentionally used a dish for a late snack and put it in the sink after she went to bed.

At bedtime, Sister had to sleep on the couch because there were only two bedrooms in the house. One was occupied by her three brothers, who slept in one bed, and the other bedroom was occupied by her father, who slept alone. She and her mother slept in the living room on a convertible, or pull-out sofa bed. Later, as she became an adolescent, another couch was purchased, but they both continued to sleep in the living room.

The father also liked dogs. He would have one or two and make the children clean up their fecal waste. Sometimes the dogs would defecate in the front yard, which was gated. The problem was that the brothers did not like cleaning it up, so when you sat on the porch or passed the house, one no doubt smelled the dog waste. You can imagine who also was responsible to clean up the ground and waste. Yes, Sister did that job as well.

As the mother and father worked in factories, she was not permitted to go to the playground after school until the house was cleaned. The mother came home about four or five in the afternoon, and then Sister had to take the two youngest siblings to the playground with her so that her mother could cook without interference. Her mother had two more girls after the youngest boy.

After dinner, it was Sister's responsibility to clean the entire kitchen for her father's inspection when he came home. Oh, did I mention that he cooked his own meals? Sister never understood why and learned not to ask questions. Guess who cleaned up his mess.

When the mother cooked for the children and herself, they sat down at the table together for their meals. They also had the best dinners on Sundays if they could afford it. There were other times when they had bean soup with a few little pieces of meat in it. Sometimes they had grits for dinner. No matter the meal, they sat down together as a family. But there was no talking at the table at mealtime. Sister, of course, was the only one to wash dishes, clean the table, and sweep the floor.

Ironically, that same table was the table the children ran around when their mother beat them with the switch, a branch from the hedges outside. This punishment was called a "whooping." It seemed the children received a beating weekly if not more often. It was her parents' rules that if one of the children did something wrong, and the neighbors told them about it, if the other siblings did not correct him or her, then whoever was involved received the whooping. Although beatings by the parents were painful, they preferred those of their mother over the father's. The father would have them remove their clothing from their waist down. They had to pull down their clothes to their ankles and then bend over on their stomachs across his bed with legs extended down the side of the bed. Then he did what they called, "tore them up." The big thick black or brown belt hurt, and their buttocks were red and scarred but not bleeding. They dared not go to the school or anywhere else and tell or show the scars.

This form of punishment was common in their culture and communities at the time. Most African American parents did these things with expectations that if the children listened, learned, and respected their rules, they would do better in life and their endeavors. The parents believed it was in their children's best interests because they did not want them to encounter trouble with the law or society.

Children during this era knew better than to inform the police or Division of Youth and Family Services about the beatings and punishments given by the parent(s). No matter how severe. There was a single parent in the community who beat her children with an iron cord. At that time, it was part of the culture and strict upbringing of some African American families.

When she was fourteen, Sister felt as though she wanted more out of life. She believed she could live a better life. She felt she had outgrown the Presbyterian church after serving as a Brownie, Girl Scout, volunteer tutor for the after-school program, and as a member of the choir. Twice she was able to go away to summer camp for a week, but she wanted more out of life.

She desired more activities and relationships. She did not want to wait until the age of eighteen. She wanted to have beautiful clothes, money, and even a boyfriend. This was during the 1970s, and love and the enjoyment of life seemed to be in the air. She saw many older couples and others in the community going out to parties, events, movies, and so on. They were dressed up and had smiles on their faces. They looked so different from her life of boredom. People seemed to enjoy their lives and each other.

In junior high school, Sister was given an opportunity to participate in the work-study program. She worked at the school, assisting teachers or administrators for about two hours a day. The salary was not much, but it provided additional assistance. For the most part, she used it to buy groceries and help her siblings. But it did not take long to realize that it really was not enough for all she desired.

Sister went looking for an after-school job. She falsified her age, saying she was sixteen when she was fourteen and looked like she was eighteen. She applied for a job at Dunkin Donuts and was hired. Although the hours were limited, the job allowed her to have additional money to purchase things for herself.

The job created an issue with her parents. Although she was providing monetary assistance to her parents and siblings, Sister thought she was what older folks referred to as, "thinking she was grown." She gave her parents problems because she felt if she were helping to take care of their family by giving them most of her earnings, the least they could do was let her enjoy life. At the time, she did not realize the restrictions were established to protect her. Sister, on the other hand, was so tired of taking care of others and wanted to enjoy and experience life.

The "being grown" journey meant going to parties, liking boys, and attending social events. She never stopped taking care of her parents and siblings, but she made sure they accepted the fact that she was adamant about, "wanting to enjoy life and wasn't looking for them to understand it or accept it because she was grown." Or so she thought.

CHAPTER THREE

While feeling grown, Sister started talking back to her
mother. She also felt she should be able to come and
go as she pleased and not only when given permission.
One day, her mother had enough of her madness. As
Sister got dressed in her new clothes, her mother ripped
them off. She tried to beat some sense into Sister. A
neighbor must have heard Sister screaming and called
the police, and when they arrived shortly thereafter,
they arrested her mother. After being bailed out from
the local precinct, she returned home that same night.
Sister was scared to say anything to her mother and
felt so bad about her arrest.

The following day, Sister experienced menstrual cramps. And in all the emotional and physical pain over her experience with her mother, she took a few Midol pills, but more than she was supposed to. She became extremely ill and had to be taken to the hospital by ambulance. She was treated and admitted.

This was her first time being hospitalized. While there, she walked down the hall of the hospital and saw a pretty black woman with long hair lying on her bed. They both said "hello." She asked Sister her name, and they had a short conversation. Later that evening, Sister took another walk and the other patient she greeted then had visitors. She asked Sister to come into her room and introduced them to each other. One man was handsome.

I will refer to him as "the man." Sister felt differently about him. It was a feeling she never felt before. He smiled, and she smiled, showing all her teeth. As she did not know why she felt this way, she excused herself and went back to her hospital room. To her surprise, as the man was leaving the hospital, he stopped by her room. There was only a brief conversation, but when he departed, he had Sister's telephone number.

She was released from the hospital the following day, and guess who called that night? It was the man.

He told her he had gone to the hospital earlier that evening, and the patient he visited told him she had been discharged. After talking for a while, Sister and her "grown self" arranged to see him the following day.

Sister was certainly not going to tell her parents that she was going to meet a man she met at the hospital. She met him around the corner of her house as he picked her up in a nice blue Monte Carlo. She still remembers the color and that feeling that she experienced. The feelings were in her heart, and they made her smile. She felt happier than ever before. She did not know how to explain it to her friends, but it was evident to them that there was something different going on in her life.

Within weeks, her mother became more curious of the phone calls and Sister going out shortly thereafter. Sister decided to tell her mother about the man. She wanted her mother to meet him and arranged it at a time when her father was at work. Sister introduced him to her mother, who immediately asked him, "How old are you?" When he told her, she responded, "Do you know how young my daughter is?" She did not hesitate to let him know that she was against their dating, especially since Sister was a minor, and he was about twenty-seven. He respectfully told her that he understood her concerns, but he wanted to date her. Sister did not dare to leave with him that night. She remembered what her mother did to her the other time she thought she was grown. She waited and later talked to her mother. She wanted her mother's approval, so while crying, Sister asked if she could date him. Her mother said no.

Days later, Sister had another conversation with her mother. She respectfully told her, "I am going to see him with or without your approval. But I really want you to approve." I think her mother was afraid that if she did not let her date him, Sister would sneak out and see him. Despite Sister's concern about going against her wishes, I do not believe her mother would have ever put her hands on her again because she was afraid to go to jail. She was also afraid of the Division of Youth and Family Services. Yes, her mother had a lot of fears. So Sister was permitted to date this man.

There was another situation that had her mother in fear. One of her mother's out-of-state relatives visited the family at least every other year. When Sister was ten years old, this cousin started telling her about a secret. The secret was that her mother's husband was not Sister's real father. Sister, not understanding this, asked her mother about it. She told Sister not to believe the cousin because he had a problem with alcohol. When he drank liquor, he talked out of his head. Since Sister did see he drank a lot of liquor when he visited and acted crazy when he did, she believed her mother.

Years later, this same cousin, during his visits, repeated this secret whether he was drunk or sober. Each time Sister wondered why he would say something like that. One day, he gave Sister a letter. He told her that it was from her real father, and he wanted her to write him. This time Sister did not tell her mother.

The letter did not say much, and it did not answer Sister's questions about the things the cousin told her. She was also confused about why the return address was from a prison in another state. Sister wrote to this person and asked, "Why is my mother's cousin saying you are my real father?" The man wrote back and responded, "I am your father."

Sister was devastated and confused. She showed her mother the letter. After reading it, her mother said, "Yes, he is your father. But if you tell anyone and your stepfather [her husband] finds out, he will kill the whole family." Sister, though not completely understanding everything, believed her mother. She did not tell her siblings.

From the time of confirmation of her biological father, Sister remained in contact with him. Her father at that time was still incarcerated, while Sister's attention and heart were given to the one who was present, the man she met at the hospital. While dating the man, she was no longer interested in attending any church. She loved him and enjoyed her life with her man. She went to parties, bars, and events with him. These were not events for teenagers; they were restricted for adults. Sister was grown, not by age, but in the new experiences of her life.

Sister was so grown she became pregnant! It broke her mother's heart. Her mother was so disappointed and embarrassed by the fact that Sister not only committed a sin, but embarrassed her parents by bearing a child, and to do such things at the age of fifteen. The birth of the child came a month after Sister's sixteenth birthday. Sister did not realize she was living a life that had not fully developed to the maturity required to raise a child.

What was even more unfortunate about all this was that when she was about seven months pregnant, the man left the state to return to his former place of residence in another state. He promised Sister he would set things up and come back and get her and his firstborn child. After she gave birth to their daughter. She called him, and he was so excited.

As Sister waited for him to set things up, they kept in contact, talking about once or twice a week via telephone. Though he was working, Sister and the baby did not receive any of his wages. One day she really expressed her anger about him not taking care of his daughter. He informed her, "I can't talk about this right now because I am getting ready for my wedding in a couple of hours!"

It took Sister some time to get through this devastation. They stopped all contact with each other. Thank God for welfare. She and the baby needed the assistance. During this era, there were many programs for teenage mothers, and she did not hesitate to enroll. She had teachers and people who did not judge her. Instead, they encouraged her to excel in life. They were of various races, genders, and ages. God also encouraged her. She enrolled in a GED program, and after two attempts at taking the test, she passed. At the age of seventeen, she was enrolled in college part time while working full time.

Sister returned to church, but this time it was a Baptist church. Although the Baptist church was about a twenty-minute walk from her house—not the few blocks away as the Presbyterian church was—she did not mind because all she really wanted was to join the youth choir. It was a new rhythm of singing and swaying to the church music. The youth sang from the choir stand while the congregation stood, sang, and sometimes shouted.

It was quite different from the Presbyterian church choir. Although she enjoyed both, she had a desire to join the Baptist church because of the singing. She was told that to be a member of the choir, you needed to be a member of the church. In order to be a member of the Baptist church, she had to be baptized. Sister did not really understand what that meant, but what she did understand was she was willing to do it to join the choir. In her mind, the church was not about being a member; it was not about being baptized. It was only about joining the choir.

After joining the church, Sister did not hesitate to go to the first choir rehearsal, which was held on a Saturday morning. There were so many children and youth there, she felt lost. No one from her neighborhood regularly attended this church. She did know one person there, but they were not friends; their parents knew one another. Sister felt discouraged and decided not to return to any more choir rehearsals.

And after about two months of attending the Sunday worship services, she stopped going to church.

About the age of seventeen, Sister went back to her former lifestyle of hanging out, partying, and having lots of fun. The first person she dated as a young single mother was one of her brother's best friends. It took her a while to even consider dating because she was so hurt and devastated by her daughter's father marrying someone else and not providing child support or consideration for either of them. Her brother's best friend will be referred to as "Bbf." He was about seventeen and well respected in the community. He was a basketball player and well known for his skills. His mother and family were also very respected.

Bbf and his family lived about ten minutes from where Sister lived. He came to the house quite often and sometimes helped Sister with her daughter. He was so helpful that while strolling with her in the carriage, some people thought he was the father. They did not see any other male so attentive, so they thought he was the father. It was evident that he loved the baby.

They dated for about six months before they broke up. Sister still saw him as her brother's friend, and not as the man who exposed her to the grown-up life she once enjoyed. Bbf, of course, was hurt. She was also hurt because he was such a special young man. She really did appreciate how he loved both her and her daughter.

Within months, she met a young man from the same city. Sister also had a part-time job checking in coats at a nightclub. One night after work, a friend gave her a ride home. In the vehicle was another passenger, whom I will refer to him as "Nb," for not biological.

Sister and Nb exchanged numbers and shortly thereafter began dating. He was another nice young man from the community whose family was well known and respected. She had concerns that his parents might have issues with their son dating someone with a child. But when she met them, they were genuinely nice. And when they met Sister's daughter, they were very loving and accepting of both. The relationship was short-lived, less than a year. But Nb and his family continued to see Sister's daughter from time to time. Nb was the first one the daughter spoke the words "da da" (Daddy).

Many other things occurred in Sister's life during this period. Maybe there will be another book to share those experiences.

CHAPTER FOUR

After being away from the church for years, Sister attended a worship service at another Baptist church in another city. It was one in which a few of her relatives were members. The first time there, she saw and heard this Baptist church choir, and again wanted to join the Baptist choir. Yes, she joined the church only to sing in its choir with her relatives. It is a well-known church and a few members were recognized gospel singers.

Sister joined this church and the choir. She enjoyed singing and looked forward to the weekly choir rehearsals. But it was not only the rehearsals. There was also the tavern where a few of them gathered after choir rehearsal. They danced, drank liquor, and had much fun. As a choir, they traveled to sing at various churches and concerts in and out of the city. It was a joyous time of her life. She enjoyed going to this church and at the same time, enjoying life.

Sister went to church almost every Sunday and seldom missed choir practice. If you asked her about the sermons preached, she most likely would not have remembered it. But if you asked her about the songs the choir sang, she would be able to tell you all about them, who sang the solo, who was crying, and what this or that person wore.

She had one foot in the church and the other in the world so to speak. During this period, she started dating a man whom she knew from times past. He will be referred to as "Bd," for baby daddy. He did not drink or go to parties or nightclubs, so they did not go out together to the places she had with former boyfriends. Bd had a different lifestyle. He would take her to New York to visit a woman he referred to as his "mom." Other times, they went to a movie or to visit one of his friends. For the most part, they spent time at Sister's apartment. She became pregnant by Bd. She left the church for a period but returned after giving birth to her second daughter.

At no time did Sister hear or feel that anyone in the church was judging her for having a second child out of wedlock. She was thankful about this, especially because when her second daughter was born, Bd was not there either. Sister had complications during the delivery of her second child, and she and the baby were ill after giving birth.

Sister was troubled and overwhelmed that she had given birth to a second child, and again, the father was not there. She did not need anyone else to judge her as she was judging herself, and it was not good, while reflecting on her life and hardships. Sister did not go back into the welfare system. Instead, she worked two jobs to take care of her children and continued to provide financially for her mother and siblings. The youngest brother, Sister babysat while he was in a cast, died of cancer at the age of eighteen.

During this time, Sister's two eldest brothers were in the military, yet Sister was the one financially supporting the family. Sister had her own apartment but because she was taking care of so many family members, she had to move back home into the first-floor apartment of her parents' two-family home. Her mother did provide babysitting for Sister's two daughters while she was working.

One day her mother and stepfather had an intense argument, and he pulled his gun on someone in the family. Everyone except the stepfather left the house, and when they returned, it was on fire. It was believed by the family that the stepfather intentionally set the house on fire. They could not prove it, but Sister yelled out her accusation as they were standing in the street, watching the flames ignited on the second floor. Although the house did not completely burn down, it was not inhabitable. It was later determined that the fire started in Sister's stepfather's bedroom. Everyone had to find a place to live. Her mother, siblings, and children initially moved to her aunt's two-bedroom apartment in another city. Her stepfather moved to another city about thirty minutes away from the house.

Sister went to her Baptist church and asked for assistance. She spoke to the secretary and informed her of the tragedy and hardship. She asked the secretary if the church would provide monetary assistance; she knew it had done so for so many others. Sister had also made many contributions to others when the church announced a person's or family's hardship and then took up a collection during Sunday worship services. She also contributed to various other church fundraisers.

The secretary said she would inform the pastor and would get back to her. She called Sister about a day or two later and told her that they had "opened the books" and found she had not been attending Sunday school or Bible study and was not a tither. It was therefore decided that the church would not take up a collection or issue a check. However, they were willing to allow her to go to the church's food panty and clothing ministry to get items to assist her and her children. Sister was so upset about what the secretary conveyed, she requested—and somewhat demanded— to speak to the pastor. The secretary promised to give him the message, but it was already discussed, and the decision was made by the pastor and church officials.

Sister never received a call from anyone else at the church, and she never returned to the church. As a matter of fact, she was so devastated by their response, that Sister did not go to church for about five years. During this period, she referred to some church folks as hypocrites. She did not intentionally disrespect the Lord, but she let her experience with that church be known to others. Sister resented church so much that she did not require her children to attend or join any church during those five years.

Sister reached out to her biological father, who was

at that time out of prison. She and her father had similar lives when it came to their parents. Sister saw her father for the first time at the age of seventeen, and it was at a prison. Her father also met his biological father for the first time at the same age. As a child, her father also believed someone else was his father. When he was informed of the truth, he found and confronted his father, who was Caucasian (an Irish man), and his father confirmed he was his biological father. As they developed a relationship as father and son, Sister's father changed his last name to that of his biological father.

Some of the relatives told Sister that her father's mother (Sister's grandmother) was put out of the family's house because of her affair with the white man (Sister's grandfather). Her grandmother was an outcast from her family because she had birthed a child by a white man in the South. They did not want the family to be subjected to prejudices and threats. Sister's great-grandmother took custody of her father when he was a child, and he barely spent time with his mother. Sister's father told her, "They found my mother in her apartment days after her death, and she died a very lonely woman." Sister's biological father was able to relate to Sister's life of secrecy and pain as well.

After the fire at her apartment, Sister called her biological father and asked him if he would ask his wife for permission to bring the girls down for the summer, so she could work two jobs and get back on her feet. Her stepmother was a blessing. She was a churchgoer, and she and Sister's father had five sons together. She loved Sister, who was the only girl on both sides of the family. The stepmother is the one who gave her the name "Sister." She was the stepbrothers only "Sister."

Although Sister's biological father and her mother committed an adulterous act that led to her birth, the stepmother did not hold it against her. The stepmother and her parents showed Sister much love, and Sister will forever remember, respect, and appreciate them.

Sister was her biological father's firstborn, but his wife was also pregnant with their first child at the same time. Her eldest stepbrother, who was the stepmother's firstborn, was born one month after Sister. In other words, her father had impregnated two women, and one carried his firstborn daughter and the other his firstborn son. The stepmother did not hesitate to call Sister and tell her to bring the girls to them. It was only for the summer, and when her daughters returned, she had an apartment.

By then Sister also had another friend, who will

be referred to as "Sm" for southern man. During this period something else occurred. Sister's former boyfriend Nb, who the oldest daughter called "da da" had married. Thereafter he was no longer actively seeing Sister's oldest daughter . Sister reflected on how the daughter's biological father was married and left them and now this other person who came into their life was also leaving. Nb had married a young lady from the same town. His wife later gave birth to their two sons. During his marriage, Nb only saw Sister's daughter about twice a year. As he was not the biological father of Sister's oldest daughter, he never financially supported her, and was not obligated to be in her life, Sister respected his marriage and family and his being distant. Nb's mother did have temporary custody of Sister's oldest daughter for a couple of months as Sister enlisted into the military. As a single parent, court proceedings for temporary custody of children was a requirement. Nb's mother was not obligated to take temporary custody as it was not her biological granddaughter. This was the type of Christian woman she was as she made many sacrifices to help others in need.

Sm was the boyfriend at this time and he assisted by providing monetary and supportive assistance as he was in love with Sister and her daughters. That relationship lasted for about a year. He later moved South of their location.

On completing her military enlistment, Sister returned home and later worked in the security profession. She worked, on average, about a sixty-four to seventy-two-hour workweek. Her job required overtime hours, which she did not refuse as she was supporting her children, mother, siblings, nieces, and nephews. This also required Sister to have someone take care of her children, and it was again her mother.

Her mother lived in the housing projects, and her two daughters spent a lot of time there. When her youngest daughter was about seven years of age, she had a friend who lived downstairs in the housing projects. The friend and her family attended church on a regular basis and sometimes a day or two during the week. One day the friend asked Sister's youngest daughter if she would like to go to church with them. She said yes and asked her grandmother. Sister's mother called her and asked if it was all right with her, and Sister said yes.

It was another Baptist church located in the same city. The church had an outreach ministry that also provided transportation. Sister's mother did not drive;

she never attempted to get a driver's license. Sister or a family member provided transportation, and a few times she would use local transportation services.

Sister's youngest daughter went to church on Wednesday nights for Bible study and on Sunday's for worship services. She also went during the week when there were special services and events at the church. Sister totally supported her attending and provided for all her financial needs. Her mother greatly assisted as she made sure Sister's youngest daughter was ready every time the bus pulled up to take her to the church or any church events.

Sister was still angry about the situation that occurred at the other church, but she continued to have respect, love, and fear of God. She did not speak disrespectful about God. It was the people who she thought were hypocrites when she attended and served in the other church. She did not consider everybody attending church to be a hypocrite, but there seemed to be more than a church should have. At least that is what she thought.

Within a few months, the youngest daughter wanted to join the church. Sister and other family members went to the church to support her during that Sunday service. Not only did Sister support her daughter, but the grandmother and Sister also joined the church that same day. Sister was so spiritually inspired that she not only enjoyed the worship service but was able to understand and relate to the preaching. For the first time, it was not about joining the choir. It was about this pastor and what he preached. And thereafter, she surrendered to God.

After Sister joined, she remembered what the Secretary said at the other Baptist church. They had found she had not done such things as attend Sunday school and Bible study. This time she made sure she attended all that was required of her, and she also became a tither. As she did, and while being more focused on learning, hearing the sermons, and being involved in the church's ministries, she felt like she was truly being born again.

There came a time when she shared the testimony with a cousin who was still a member of the church of the "open books." The pastor of that church had since retired but to Sister's amazement, her cousin was still in contact with him. Her cousin was so overjoyed with Sister's spiritual growth and transformation that she asked if she could call the pastor and tell him.

Sister was so elated and grateful that her cousin offered because she wanted to let him know but did not have a contact telephone number to tell him. The cousin called him while Sister was at the house, and she allowed Sister to speak to him and give her testimony. She reminded the pastor of her prior experience at his church and informed him of her recent Christian conversion, transformation, and development. She thanked him and expressed her appreciation and respect for his leadership and shepherding. He thanked her for the testimony and wished her well in her Christian journey.

That same year, the pastor died. He left his earthly vessel and went on to be with the Lord. That chosen pastor was someone she believed God had her to come to know as one who truly was called by Him to equip the church under the fivefold ministry as stated in Ephesians 4:11–31. Sister did not initially understand his leadership, but as she grew spiritually, she appreciated and respected him even more. He did not compromise the Word of God or the foundational church principles as ordained by God. He attempted to guide her and others on the straight and narrow path of God's righteousness. At that time, she was unknowingly traveling the broad path led by her lack of knowledge, wisdom, or understanding of the Word of God.

Blessed are those who are persecuted because of righteousness, for theirs is the kingdom of heaven. (Matthew 5:10)

The more Sister desired to learn about God and being a born-again Christian, the more she encountered rejection from family, friends, associates, and church folk. These are a few examples of those experiences.

FAMILY

Sister was attempting to repent from her past, draw closer to the Lord, and be more Christlike. This was early in her transitional stages after joining the Baptist church in her city.

For the most part, her family, friends, and associates were not believing, seeing, or feeling it. They made sure to keep reminding her of her past sinful life. It was not as if they were referring to criminal acts of a sinful life but to a life of basic pleasures and excitement as temptations of the world were available for her and others to enjoy.

She mentioned the times she visited her father and family in the South. She enjoyed hanging out with her biological father and drinking socially at the little clubhouses. In the beginning stage of her Christian transitioning, she attended the clubs and drank cherry keeyafa while engaging in conversation. At times, she discussed religion and proudly revealed that she was a Christian.

While there, she also attempted to lead a few people unto the Lord. It seemed she was evangelizing while socializing. Before long, the Spirit of God convicted her, and she stopped going to the clubhouse. Christians can drink but not in excess (1 Corinthians 5:11). They can also socialize but are to be mindful of their demeanor. Sister did not want to drink any form of alcoholic beverage and unintentionally say something that was contrary to the Word of God. She did not want to mislead anyone or give the wrong impression. She was growing by grace and was a babe in Christ Jesus.

Her father respected her conversion, but he let her know he missed the days that they hung out together, drinking and having fun. Sister missed them, too, as they did not have many conversations about religion after she decided to abstain. Her father had just started attending church and sat in the back pew, playing with the little children who also sat in the back. She was so glad that he returned to church and thankful unto God that she was sometimes able to sit with him.

It meant so much to have a parent in church with the young or adult children. Sister's stepmother was a faithful servant and member of the AME (African Methodist Episcopal) church. She was not only a hearer but a doer of the Word of God. She was a blessing to Sister as she treated her like a daughter. In over forty years of knowing one another, Sister and her stepmother had only one argument. It extended from a discussion about Sister wanting her father to drive the three of them to church as a family. Her father and stepmother always drove to church in separate cars.

The request was made when the stepmother was diagnosed with cancer, and Sister traveled back and forth by plane to be there for her. This time, Sister saw that she seemed to be declining in health and might not be healed as readily as thought. She did not know how soon she would return to their house again, but she considered her stepmother might pass before she returned in a month or so. Sister longed for this family ride to church, even before her stepmother became ill. It never occurred.

About two weeks after Sister returned home, her stepmother passed on to be with the Lord.

OLDEST DAUGHTER

Sister's oldest daughter was in her early teens during Sister's initial reunification with a Baptist church. The daughter rejected her mother's transition into Christianity and Sister's attempts to transition her as well. The grandmother had the daughter at her house while Sister worked. The daughter later moved in with the grandmother during a stage of serious rebellion.

This was not the youngest daughter, who initially joined the Baptist church. It was her sister. In all fairness to her eldest daughter, Sister felt that it was her fault as the mother. She waited until the child was about twelve years old before she mandated that she attend church on a regular basis.

At the same time, the daughter was seeing the world in a different light, the lifestyle that Sister once lived. The lifestyle she became accustomed to prior to her mother's returning to church. It was being in the world and enjoying the pleasures of life. She was behaving like a normal teenager.

Sister did not know how to transition her daughter other than to say, "I am your mother, and you do as you're told." As Sister's efforts to transition her oldest daughter did not work, she went to the church's youth pastor.

Thank God he took the time to minister to her daughter. The senior pastor ministered to the family as they were transitioning. The church also prayed for the family.

Sister's daughter tried to change, but eventually stopped going to church as she was residing with her grandmother. The grandmother did not require that she attend church. She was the same age Sister was when her mother no longer mandated that she attend church as a teenager.

Sister was the primary provider for the family, and with a hectic work schedule, she could not be home to provide the quality time and upbringing that she wanted for her daughters. Therefore, she had to allow her mother to watch and somewhat raise them. This was one of the most difficult things a parent must decide to do. But at the same time, you make decisions based on what you believe is best as you take all things into consideration. You attempt to make the best of it and pray for the best outcome.

Sister is thankful her mother and other family members were there to assist with her daughters. Sister paid a substantial cost monetarily and physically as she worked numerous hours to take care of her children, mother, and many other family members for most of her adult life.

FRIENDS AND ASSOCIATES

During this time, Sister had few friends and associates. She had not made connections with the members of the church of her new conversion. She had one female special friend in the community with whom she was close. The relationship was as though they were sisters. But after ten years, they parted ways, and each had a lot of hostility toward the other. As a matter of fact, a week or two after Sister joined the church, they had a physical fight in the middle of the street and in front of Sister's youngest daughter and others.

Sister called the new pastor and informed him what occurred. He was not pleased. He told her to repent, ask God for forgiveness, and apologize to her friend. Sister was willing to ask God for forgiveness, but she did not feel she should apologize to or forgive the friend. Sister did not call her.

Months later, Sister was in Bible study, and the pastor taught about forgiveness. The Spirit of God convicted her, and after Bible study that night, Sister went to her former friend's house. The mother of the friend came to the door. Sister told her what she learned in Bible study and said, "I came to apologize."

The friend's mother said, "I know that must be God because some people go to church and would have not done that." She accepted the apology on behalf of her daughter, who was not at home at the time. The former friend called Sister later that night, and they began to reconnect on speaking terms.

MALE FRIEND AND LOVER

Sister recalled a night she was at work and reading 1 Thessalonians 4:3, 4 and Ephesians 5:3. She read about fornication and found a dictionary. After reading the definition, she told herself, "That is what I am doing!"

Fornication, as defined by the *American Heritage Dictionary*, is, "Sexual intercourse between a man and a woman not married to each other." She felt so bad inside. Sister had just committed this act with her male companion prior to coming to work. Initially she felt good about the relationship. Until she read the scripture and definition.

It was not as if she did not know it was a sin prior to this night. She had two children out of wedlock and had other former boyfriends. But for whatever reason on this night and at this time, she was convicted to the core of hypocrisy in her religious and spiritual conversions.

In her spiritual conviction, she called her fornicating male friend before leaving her job. She told him, "I need to talk to you about something, and it is urgent that I see you as soon as I finish work."

He consented, and when she left her job, she went back to his house; they did not live together. Mind you, he was also a Christian and served at another Baptist church. Sister showed him the passage of scripture and told him how the Holy Spirit convicted her. His response was, "You were convicted, but I was not."

Sister told him she could no longer have that type of relationship with him. He let her know that he was an older man, and God gave him some needs. And if she thought that he would stop, she was talking to the wrong man!

Well, that ended that relationship as such. It was a very painful loss to her as she absolutely loved this man, or so she felt and thought. Sister did not understand why God did not work this out. She would have married him in order to have the relationship approved by God.

Sister later found out that all along he was dating other women, and he was happy in his lust. She thanked God for big favors as he separated them. God revealed to her she deserved and was worth more, especially in her new and saved life in Christ Jesus.

CHAPTER FIVE

Marriage

As she learned more about fornication, she made another major decision. In her carnal mind, Sister did not believe that she could become celibate by abstaining from sexual intercourse. She did not envision or understand how anyone could live a normal life while being in a long period of celibacy.

During this era, she thought if a female did not have a boyfriend or was not dating, she was looked on as one possibly having a secretive health issue or disease that would not allow her to have sexual relationships or companionship. She also believed a woman's identity and respect had much to do with her interaction with the opposite sex.

Consequently, she began to think about how to have a relationship with a male and it be pleasing to her and approved by God. She thought that as a young woman, she should not be without male companionship or commitment. She considered marriage. Of course, it would not be with a stranger. She asked herself, "Who?" and, "When?"

Mind you, she was a new member of the Baptist church and growing in the Lord. She also wanted to do right in the Lord. For some reason, she thought about her sin of the births of her daughters while fornicating. She believed she still needed to correct those past sins. God knows she did not see her daughters as the sin, but the sexual acts outside of marriage were the sins.

Sister did not know or fully understand the scriptures, "If we confess our sins, he is faithful and just to forgive us our sins, and to cleanse us from all unrighteousness" (1 John 1:9), or, "If any man (human) be in Christ, he is a new creature; old things are passed away, behold, all things are become anew (2 Corinthians 5:17).

Sister was reading and learning a lot from other religious texts. Yet what she did not realize at the time was that she should have taken baby steps. She was applying the literal application of her readings without their Spiritual relevance, understanding, and development. She was reading passages and books on her own and taking the writings out of context while attempting to apply them to her life without the appropriate knowledge of the text or their application. She did not even know how to go to the pastor or the designated person(s) in the church to ask for further instruction or counsel.

She learned later that if she had consulted with her pastor or some of the assigned officials of the church, then she would not have been confused about some things. This is another reason it is important that the people of God not only attend church but utilize the ministries as offered by the church. Christians need to engage in the teaching and relationship ministries that help us in our development. In addition to Sunday school and Bible study, the saints should also participate in the conventions, church meetings, and so on.

NOT FORGIVING YOURSELF

As Sister wanted to be right in the eyes of God and others, she reached out to her oldest daughter's biological father, who was living in a state south of where she was living. Never mind he only saw his daughter once in her twelve years of life and did not provide any child support.

This was the man who, during their former relationship, Sister believed she would marry before she became pregnant. Sister, in her telephone search, contacted one of his relatives. She was told that he was divorced and living with the family member Sister had called. Sister gave her number to his cousin and asked that he call her. He called the following day. After that day, he called every day.

They had several in-depth telephone conversations regarding what seemed to be his sincere remorse in failing her as a boyfriend and even more as a father to their daughter. They talked not only every day but two or three times a day while both living in separate states.

Also, during this same time, Sister was also dating a man who will be referred to as "Uy" as they were unequally yoked. They were not only dating but living together. Yes, Sister had broken up with one man because of fornication and later found herself in another relationship with the same sinful act. This is referred to as backsliding; it occurs when someone reverts to his or her sinful ways of the past.

When she initially started dating Uy, she was not attending church. When their relationship developed over a period, he moved in with her. They eventually lived together in one of the two homes that she owned. Yes, it was her house and mortgage, but Uy assisted with the expenses.

They started dating while she was residing in her first home. He moved in with her after she sold the first home and purchased another. While living together, Sister joined the Baptist church in her city. This was the church where she felt that she was born again. As she was regularly attending church again, she started being more attentive to hearing and learning the Word of God.

As such, she was having more convictions of her past and present sins. The convictions were personal and relational. She even realized she was not properly training her children in accordance to the Word of God (Proverbs 29:21).

Uy loved Sister's daughters, and they loved him.

The problem was that he was not going to church and had no desire to partake of it. Well, for the first time in her life, Sister had her fill of hearing the Baptist pastor preach and teach about fornication, shacking, and sins. Sister felt convictions from within, and it did not feel good. Uy's love was gratifying, but it was not such that she was willing to continue to live a life of hypocrisy. Sister had been there and done that too long. She felt she needed to make some decisions regarding her relationship with Uy and God.

She had a few serious discussions with Uy, and he still was not ready to convert. Consequently, Sister made the decision to break off the relationship. She told him, "I want to do that which was right in the Lord and as a Christian." The children were confused and hurt because they really loved him.

One day while talking long distance to the man, her oldest daughter's father, she shared her thoughts with him about her sincere desire to adhere to the Word of God. He also expressed how he wanted to do that which is right in the Lord. He was divorced and lonely, and he welcomed another chance with her and the children.

He also felt that this would be an opportunity for him to do what he should have done when they were initially together. He hoped it would also allow him to be the father to their daughter, which he should have been from the beginning.

This was surely thought of as a blessing to Sister as he and she could both now be right with the Lord. They both wanted to be seen right in the eyes of their daughter, who referred to her father as the one having neglected her. It was also an opportunity for both daughters to see their mother repent and attempt to live life according to the Word of God.

The man also promised to love the youngest daughter and be a family man of God to her as well. He spoke of all the Spiritual and emotional things Sister wanted, needed, and longed to hear.

Within a short period, she informed Uy that she was in contact with her oldest daughter's father. He did not take Sister's spiritual transition seriously. By that time, she was ready to move on, so she asked him to move out. He asked for two to four weeks to move, and she agreed. In the meantime, she continued her communications with the man.

Uy was aware of their calls and her plans to go to visit the man. Before she departed to visit him and possibly reconnect, the man called her and asked her to marry him. She said yes.

Sister called her church to tell her pastor, but he was not available. She informed the secretary that she would be getting married. The secretary asked if she wanted an appointment with the pastor for premarital counseling. Sister told her that it was not necessary because she was doing what was written in the Bible (Hebrews 13:4).

Within a couple of weeks, Sister and her oldest daughter were traveling by plane to see the man. She did not tell any of her family members what she was about to do. She did not tell her daughter until they were at the airport waiting for the flight to depart.

When she told her, the daughter said, "Mommy, how are you going to marry him when you haven't been with him for all these years?" Sister attempted to explain it from the biblical perspective, but her daughter was still confused. She thought she understood her daughter's confusion but had no idea how the overall impact of this news affected her at that time or in the future.

The man had two adolescent children by his former wife, and they also lived in the same state where Sister was visiting him. His son was initially more accepting of the wedding announcement, but his daughter was totally devastated and against her father being with another woman.

Sister's daughter and her stepdaughter cried at the wedding, which was two days after their arrival. A day after the wedding, she and her daughter returned to their home state because Sister's employer would not approve of any extended time off from work. That was unfortunate yet not so devastating because she had other plans.

Sister was so serious about her life as a Christian that she had decided to give her fully furnished one family house to the Baptist church and move to the state where he resided. As she had an outstanding debt on the house, her plans were to turn over the house to the church, the church would sell the house, and then the church would keep the full profit from the sale.

When she returned from her wedding, she finalized the plan with the church, gave her two-week notice to her employer, sent in an application to a job listing in the other state, and addressed all other matters that needed taken care of before her departure.

Uy moved out a couple of days after she returned home and after Sister told him she was married. Within weeks, her husband flew in for a couple of days to assist his wife's move to her new home. He also went to city hall to sign their daughter's birth certificate. Prior to this, his name as her father was not permitted to be stated on the birth certificate because at the time of the birth, he was not physically there to sign the birth certificate as required by the hospital.

Both Sister and her husband discussed it before and after their wedding. When he came to assist with the moving, the signature was planned and discussed with their daughter. At that time, she had not stated any objections.

The only thing Sister took out of the house when moving were her clothes and personal documents. She placed them in her vehicle and then turned the house keys over to the church. She drove over ten hours to her new residence with her husband. Her daughters remained in New Jersey with her mother as Sister needed to prepare and plan for their move.

Unfortunately, after her departure there was a change in the economy. There was a period of economic depression, and the housing market suffered. The church was not able to sell the house as planned. They rented it for a period, but there were situations that complicated the plan.

Although Sister's intentions were spiritually motivated, she later realized she had no other option but to have the house go into foreclosure. The bank did foreclose on the property.

To this day, Sister has never had any second thoughts or regrets about the transactions she made with the church.

CHAPTER SIX

Sister's New Location

As Sister was transitioning to her new location, she felt it would be better for her daughters to stay with their grandmother until she could prepare for them to join her. Within a period of two months, Sister was thanking God that she did not have her children there because her life was in a state of turmoil.

Sister's oldest daughter was right: she really did not know him. Her husband was a functioning alcoholic. He drank two to four tall cans of beer every day. He was able to maintain a full-time job as a supervisor in the auto parts industry. She did not believe he drank beer while working, and there were never any disciplinary actions against him for any alcohol-related incidents. He was well liked and respected by most. He was well received by customers and the general public.

The problem was when he got off from work and on his days off. He was a different person after drinking beer. There were no physical issues, yet the difference was emotionally painful to encounter and a problem for both. During this period, Sister did not drink any alcoholic beverages, so the smell and taste of the beer from him was offensive to her. Occasionally was tolerable, but every day was unbearable.

Their marriage was his second and her first. Sister did not know how to respond to her marital problems, the stepchildren, and his former spouse. Unknown to Sister, his former wife had a court action against him for substantial arrears in child support payments. Within the first month of his marriage to Sister, his salary was garnished, and payroll deductions had him in poverty. It was so much that he could not afford the monthly rent and utilities for the apartment he newly leased for him and his new wife.

Sister, on the other hand, had her own issues. She thought she would be working in a matter of weeks as she had applied for the job in her new state before arriving. On arrival, she believed it was only a matter of completing the employment process. But the process was taking longer than expected, so Sister had to live off her credit cards because her husband could not support her. The credit cards were being used to their maximums because she had other outstanding debts. There were at least eight major credit cards. She did not begin working until about four months after her arrival.

Sister was so overwhelmed with all that she was encountering, she did not tell her family or friends. What they did know was that she was calling them for financial assistance, and they did not understand. Prior to her moving, they already thought she had lost her mind when she turned over her house to the church, married her daughter's father, resigned her job, and moved to another state.

Sister finally went to the pastor of the church they attended. It was an AME church her husband's family attended. The pastor counseled and prayed for them. Unfortunately, it seemed unsuccessful because the couple's marital problems and issues continued to spiral without resolutions.

As much as Sister tried to be patient, loving, and encouraging, she found that her husband needed professional help with so many issues he had not addressed since childhood. Sister was so drained with it all. She left him twice and drove over ten hours alone to return to her mother's home. Each time she left, she returned to him because she believed it was the Christian thing to do. Eventually there came a time, as things continued to spiral and their marriage was very much in trouble, Sister did not believe God wanted her to remain in their state of chaos.

It was less than three years of marriage. Her father and brother came to where she and her husband were residing. Sister told her brother that she was leaving her husband for the final time and needed some help to move back to her former state. She was going to stay with her mother until she found an apartment.

Her brother told their father. Sister did not know he had contacted her father until they both arrived at the apartment to help her leave. It was about a six-hour ride for the father and brother to drive there. Her father had a rifle and a pistol in his car. He did not pull them out and aim them at her husband, but when the man came outside to talk to them, Sister's father opened the trunk to let him see them—just in case he didn't understand her father was serious.

Her father put her belongings in his vehicle, took her to the airport, and told her not go come back to her husband or that state.

About a year after returning to her former state, Sister divorced her husband. She did not consider it all her former husband's fault. It was a combination of many things.

Sister returned home and to the Baptist church that was first attended by her youngest daughter. She believed that God could have saved their marriage if her husband and she had let Him take control. It was then that she realized she did not understand the true essence of the marital vows of the sanctity of marriage in accordance to the Word of God.

Her former husband later married again, and this was his third marriage. He later separated from his wife. He is now deceased. Sister thanks God that she and he reconciled their differences a year or so after their divorce and years before his death. She also visited him while he was ill from the effects of the alcohol.

Sister was also thankful that her once rebellious daughter forgave her biological father for not being there for her. As an adult, she also returned to church. In her Christian development, she went to spend some time with him before his death. He also came to New Jersey to spend time with her and had an opportunity to see his grandson. When he passed, their daughter attended his funeral service. Sister remains in contact with some of her former in-laws and family members, whom she continues to love very much.

Sister remembered a phone call her former husband made to Nb. He conveyed his gratitude to Nb, who gave so much of himself to be like a father to his daughter when he, the biological father, failed to do so. He also respected their relationship and thought that he had no right to interfere or attempt to expect his daughter to dissolve it for his sake. Her biological father was thankful that their daughter permitted him opportunities to spend time with her, although he felt that he really did not deserve her forgiveness.

Sister was so thankful to God that their daughter, in the Spirit of Christ Jesus, prevailed throughout this whole matter as she seemed to forgive her father's faults. Her father really needed the forgiveness of God and his daughter.

CHAPTER SEVEN

Repented Life

After Sister divorced her husband and returned to the church in surrender to the biblical teachings, she has not fornicated or lived with another male. That was over eight years ago. You may wonder if she has had a relationship with a female. Her answer: no. Sister states she never has had a desire for an intimate relationship with any female. She further states, "This is not said in judgment or condemnation. It is my sincere truth and life."

When considering the other devices on the market being used for sexual gratification, the question was asked, "Has Sister purchased or used such devices?" Her response: no.

Sister attributes her not engaging in the lust and temptations of sexual activity as a gift given by God. Through her belief and faith in God the Father, Son, and Holy Spirit, she has a higher regard for her life as a woman and daughter of the Most High God. She wants to date and marry one day, but she is determined to wait until God reveals and sends His chosen man for her to wed.

This can be inspiring to females who believe they must participate in the world's status quo by being sexually active. Lately, there has been much exposure and a sense of endorsement for those who openly identify themselves as a lesbian, female escort, bisexual, and various other sexual identities and relationships. This is their prerogative.

On the other hand, there is one classification that has received extremely limited coverage. Being single and a virgin is a blessing, and not a curse. Our society and churches should provide more awareness of these issues in the contexts of world exposure and sacred doctrines. If there are pastors uncomfortable preaching and teaching abstinence, they should consider how they are not equipping the church in accordance with Ephesians 4:11–24. Also, the scriptures as written in 2 Timothy 3:16–17 and Matthew 28:19–20 are relevant.

> All scripture is God-breathed and is useful for teaching, rebuking, correcting and training in righteousness, so that the servant of God may be thoroughly equipped for every good work. (2 Timothy 3:16–17)

> Therefore go and make disciples of all nations, baptizing them in the name of the Father and of the Son and of the Holy Spirit, and teaching them to obey everything I have commanded you. And surely I am with you always, to the very end of the age. (Matthew 28:19–20)

CHAPTER EIGHT

So Christ himself gave the apostles, the prophets, the evangelists, the pastors and teachers, to equip his people for works of service, so that the body of Christ may be built up until we all reach unity in the faith and in the knowledge of the Son of God and become mature, attaining to the whole measure of the fullness of Christ. (Ephesians 4:11–13)

CALL TO MINISTRY

After the divorce, Sister joined a church that she became familiar with while observing the worship services as provided to others. It was a Pentecostal church located in the same township. Their pastor was a bishop and the founder of that church.

Sister visited the church and later joined. Later, the bishop licensed her as an evangelist. She served in the prison ministry for about four years. During that time, she served with the ministry team that provided religious services to the women's correctional prison, a male diagnostic center for sex offenders, and the men's prison. She also assisted with outreach ministries, feeding of the poor, and assisting the bishop in other services of ministry.

There came a time when she felt led to return to the Baptist church. She had a discussion with the bishop and gave her his blessing. He also permitted her to continue with the prison ministries schedule. Sister then joined the Baptist church of the pastor of the church her youngest daughter attended.

During this period, the Baptist pastor was at another location in another city. Sister reflected on all that she had learned and transitioned in her Christian faith when he was her pastor. Therefore, she did not mind driving between twenty and thirty minutes to attend the church.

Within months, Sister joined this Baptist church. Prior to her joining, her mother, siblings, and adult daughters were not attending church. After she reunited with this pastor and joined the church, the family members attended and became members. Sister had an aunt, her mother's sister, who also joined and attended almost every week. Their attendance was more than Sunday worship services. They also attended Bible study. And most of the family members were tithers.

During Sister's first year of membership at the Baptist church, she occasionally visited the Pentecostal church. One day the Bishop requested to have a meeting with her regarding her call to ministry. He informed her that the Spirit of God had spoken to him and revealed that God was placing her at a higher level in ministry. It was time for her to be elevated as an ordained minister.

Sister was shocked because she also believed that God was revealing something unto her, and it pertained to being elevated. She had not shared it with anyone because she wanted to be sure it was God. To her, this was confirmation.

This was complicated. At that time, she was a

member of a Baptist church, and the bishop presided over the Pentecostal church. She and the bishop agreed that she should discuss this with her Baptist pastor. Even more complicated, Sister knew that the Baptist pastor would most likely not approve of her being ordained for various reasons.

The Baptist pastor had not witnessed Sister serving in the prisons and the other services in her call to ministry. When she discussed this with him, he politely responded in the manner she expected. He did not approve of her ordination by the bishop. He would not even recognize her as a licensed evangelist or minister. It was a difficult period for Sister.

At this same Baptist church, the pastor was aware at his church she was serving with the Women's Ministry, missionaries, Outreach Ministry, Grandparents Raising Grandchildren Ministry, and Prayer Ministry. The pastor had publicly acknowledged his belief that women should not serve as clergy. Sister attempted to respect his position, but at the same time, she felt she had to foremost revere and respect what was willed by the Lord God Almighty.

Sister struggled with this for months and knew she needed to have meeting with her pastor. She also remembered during this period that there were innumerable times when this Baptist pastor preached a sermon from a passage that the Spirit of God gave her earlier that week. There were other times that the pastor said things the Spirit of God ministered to her also during the week. It did not just happen a few times but so many until one day, while in Sunday worship service at her Baptist church, which was a Mega church, it occurred again.

This time, Sister got up from her seated position in the pew and started running around the church while the pastor was preaching. There were other Sunday worship services during which she ran, shouted, and cried aloud. She felt as though she was experiencing, "His word is in my heart like a fire, a fire shut up in my bones" (Jeremiah 20:9b).

If anyone had told her or suggested that she would ever run around a megachurch, she would deny the thought and consider it an embarrassment. The issue was that this was not about her and others but about her and God. As much as she wanted to stop, she could not at that time. She thought that the Spirit of God was speaking to her, and the confirmations spoken and preached by a phenomenal pastor and teacher had her in another Spiritual realm that even she did not understand at that time.

Realizing that the pastor, did not understand what she was encountering Spiritually, she believed that she had to decide to either except the ordination by the Pentecostal bishop or wait for the Baptist pastor (2 Peter 1:10).

She did meet with the pastor of the Baptist Church and he disapproved of her being licensed or ordained.

She wrestled with the thought of waiting on what she believed at that time was man's confirmation or proceed in obedience to what she believed was confirmation by God. She consequently surrendered and went forth and was ordained by the Bishop.

This caused many problems for her as a member of the Baptist church. Sister did not know the ramifications of it all until after she was ordained. She later felt that she in effect disrespected the pastor, the official board, church bylaws, and the Baptist doctrine. Sister thereafter learned that if she genuinely believed God had spoken this, she could have, in respect to all involved, left the Baptist church and returned to the church of the Pentecostal bishop. Sister later realized what she did by receiving the ordination and continuing her membership at the Baptist church was out of order.

Thank God for His mercy and grace because the

Baptist pastor could have subjected her to many forms of discipline and the possible recommendation of unfavorable standing as a member of the church.

I also believe what was favorable on Sister's behalf was that she never asked the Baptist pastor to allow her to serve as a minister at the Baptist church. Nor did she ask to be recognized by the congregants as a minister on staff at the Baptist church. Sister just wanted the pastor's blessing on her pursuit and call to ministry. When she met with him, she cried as she informed him of her desire to receive his blessing, but he politely denied the request. Ten years after her ordination, he still refers to her as "Sister" and does not refer to her as a minister. Recently, this Baptist pastor ordained his daughter, wife, and two other women clergy. He refers to those he licensed and ordained as "Reverend."

Regardless, Sister has continued to have the upmost respect for the pastor. She had so much respect that when she realized the conflict, she left the Baptist church and reunited with the Pentecostal church.

While serving with the bishop and yet still desiring to be a member of a Baptist church, Sister met a female pastor who was appointed to a Baptist church in her city. At that time, she was the only any female Baptist pastor. According to Sister, it was, "Nothing short of a miracle."

Sister did not hesitate to discuss her desires with her bishop and the female Baptist pastor. The two pastors knew each other, and they agreed Sister would leave the Pentecostal church and become a member of the Baptist church.

The pastor at the Baptist church had a full-time day job, so Sister, while serving as an associate minister was given many opportunities to serve the church during the day. For example, she officiated Noon Day Prayer; visited the sick at home, hospitals, convalescent homes, and other locations; followed up on urgent calls to the church; and other assignments as given by the pastor. She assisted in the pulpit for all worship services, funerals, and other services as required.

This Baptist church also united with other churches in the city. A Baptist church under reconstruction temporarily had their services at a community center. They did not have a female minister, but unlike the former Baptist church pastor, this pastor wanted female clergy. Sister was asked if she would be willing to help prepare the female candidates chosen by the church to give their initial sermon" in their call to ministry. It was discussed and approved by both pastors. Sister, to better assist the other Baptist church, also joined them and remained with them for about a year.

Another Baptist church in the same city had two associate ministers. One of them was a candidate to pastor another church. The other associate minister was temporarily leaving to serve foreign missions. This was another opportunity for Sister to assist a pastor and serve her call to ministry.

Sister served in all these churches without pay. She also had a full-time job but worked the third shift. All the services that she provided to these churches was done on a voluntary basis. She not only served but continued to attend each church's Sunday worship service, Sunday school, Bible study, church ministries, and events. She was also a tither in each church and provided additional and substantial contributions to these churches.

Unfortunately, Sister was referred by some as a "church hopper." Regardless of all the ministerial services that the Lord provided through her, some people questioned why she moved from church to church. Most people in these communities were not aware of the underlying reasons Sister moved from church to church. To some churchgoers, she was not seen as a stable church member. The pastors knew the circumstances, but they were not openly discussed with the congregants or the general public. Consequently, Sister encountered many forms of judgment as many Christians believe that a congregant's term, or period of membership, at a church reflects your dedication and/or commitment to Christianity and the church.

God, who is the author and finisher of her faith, kept Sister on course. Through it all, the Lord had her to enroll in a Bible college while working and serving as an associate minister to these churches. For three years, she traveled once a week from her state to another state while working and providing services to these churches to pursue and obtain a bachelor's degree in Bible.

Thereafter, she continued her studies at a seminary and obtained her Master of Divinity in theology. While matriculating at the seminary, she was required to complete an internship. The Baptist church she was serving as an associate minister at that time was not able to meet the seminary's requirements for the internship because the pastor was ill for an extended period.

Sister therefore left that church and joined another Baptist church that was able to provide a full-time pastor who would oversee the required internship training and degree requirements. This was another topic for others to discuss about Sister because some Christians continued to judge her as attending yet another church. They had no understanding that she had to pursue other methods to complete the required courses and training for the Master of Divinity degree.

After being a member of that Baptist church for about two years, the senior pastor ordained Sister to the continued work of the Gospel Ministry after she was approved by the Ordaining Council of the Baptist Church and Association. There would no longer be an issue of her being an ordained minister by the Pentecostal church while serving as a minister of the Baptist church.

About a year after her ordination, Sister moved to another state. While looking for a Baptist church to serve, she initially attended her family's AME church. She later joined a Baptist church and served as an associate minister, a Bible study teacher, Sunday school teacher assistant, and an aide to Children's Ministry.

She attended and joined the Baptist church akin to the one that "opened the books." The pastor was like the pastor who had the books opened. She had such a high regard for this pastor's leadership and under-shepherding, which she believed were given and ordained by God.

Some pastors are called to serve a church by methods contrary to the Word of God. There is a difference between serving by the call of humankind and serving by the call of God (Hebrews 5:1–4; 2 Peter 1–3; Jeremiah 1:5).

Sister believes that God allowed her to go through all these life experiences to better serve Him and others. She believes that until Christians study, learn, and adhere to the Holy Bible, they will not acquire the wholesome life granted by God and given in the life, death, resurrection, ascension, and reign of Christ Jesus. It is a life revealed in the writings of the Holy Bible and inspired by the Holy Spirit of God.

Sister found that in many churches, less than one third of the membership attended Sunday school, Bible study, and other ministries that are needed for spiritual growth. It is written, "My people are destroyed from lack of knowledge" (Hosea 6a). It was not as though some pastors were not encouraging and providing the biblical references to the need for everyone to attend the various ministries and teachings.

For whatever reason, Christians throughout various denominations and churches believe this is not required for their Christian lives. Sister understood their misunderstandings as in the past, she also had that mindset. She was thankful for once being spiritually blind but then being able to see (John 9:25).

Sister's singing in the church choirs, although a blessing, did not and could not provide her with the foundational teachings and necessities for her Spiritual growth and development. As she studied, engaged, and learned about biblical writings, it did not circumvent her trials and tribulations, but it helped to guide her through each situation. She came to better understand what is referred to as the Great Commission, as Jesus Christ commissioned the apostles to "go and make disciples of all nations, baptizing, them in the name of the Father And of the Son and of the Holy Spirit, and teaching them to obey everything I have Commanded you. And surely, I am with you always, to the very end of age" (Matthew 28:19–20).

The choir's songs could not rescue her from her day-to-day occurrences and issues. Singing some of the contemporary religious songs were emotionally stimulating, and the traditional hymns were spiritually stimulating. Sister realized the Word of God was vital and essential as a reference for a wholesome Christian life.

Sister was concerned about the televised broadcasts of church services. "Surely, we are to make a joyful noise unto the Lord and enter His gates with Thanksgiving and praise" (Psalm 100:1–5). Her question and concern, "Are we really worshipping and praising God in the manner that is pleasing to Him? Are the worship services developed and conducted as an assembly for church or entertainment? Are the songs as written and directed for the congregants to sing in church, written and inspired by the carnal mind for individual fame? Is it emotionalism or spiritualism?"

The questions are not asked in judgment or condemnation but to determine whether the church one attends or is considering attending, is aligned with the Word of God.

In His house of prayer—the church—what is being preached and taught? In former years, pastors preached from Genesis to Revelation and would not hesitate to state, "Thus sayeth the Lord!"

For the last decade or so, sermons and teachings are preached more from New Testament writings and less from the Old Testament. History is becoming more and more irrelevant to adults, children, families, society, and life application. The less respect and appreciation people have for it, the more they ignore the developments, especially as they relate to biblical historical context and application.

More Pastors are requesting congregants to engage more in Sunday Worship Services by giving high-fives, turning to the next person and repeating or speak things into other people's lives, and embracing three people or more. This is especially true when the service is being televised. In some churches, if you do not comply, the music leaders or pastors will call people out and depict them as not honoring God.

This is not biblical, and no church attendee should be made to perform such in order to be accepted or respected by the church. Everyone should be permitted to participate in a manner that is respectful. That includes respectfully just sitting quietly as they attentively listen to what is being taught or preached. Some preachers seemingly want more people to yell aloud with, "Amen," or, "Preach, Pastor." Some church services seem to be in order or appearance of a social gathering than a gathering of Saints. Perhaps that is why there is a trend of people dressing as if they were going to a nightclub and some who wear revealing attire. Unfortunately, these are the times when you dare not speak truth to anyone, including some pastors. Who wants to hear, "Respect the house of the Lord our God?"

What is the biblical story of the church? What is your story while being a part of the church?

This is a question Sister asked herself. Her story is told because she hopes it can help others to realize that everyone has a story and a journey. If you will consider taking the time to study and learn the story of the Sovereign God and Father as established in the biblical writings from Genesis to Revelation, and in faith join in covenant with Him through His Son, our Savior Jesus Christ, you will be rewarded with a life that no other can give or take away. You will be made wholesome with the life, love, grace, and mercy that only God can give through a relationship with Him.

Once you go through various transformations in your Spiritual development, there will be no regrets as you acquire the knowledge of the love of God that surpasses mere comprehension. As you receive it, you will most likely in gratitude serve God, the church, and others. You will have a profound understanding, appreciation, and respect for the God who so loved the world that He gave His only begotten Son (John 3:16).

Our Sovereign God honors His Son in the highest regard. He does not approve of anyone or anything that demeans the ultimate sacrifice and atonement that His Son gave for us all. Expecting God to denounce the accomplishments of His Son is against what is established by God, the Creator of heaven and earth. We can receive

Jesus Christ in disproportion to limit desires to know and receive Him, or we can receive Him according to the love of our Sovereign Father God, who blessed us with the best gift we will ever receive in our lives or deaths. Choose for yourselves this day whom you will serve (Joshua 24:15).

As Sister gives her testimony regarding her trials and tribulations, she also makes it clear that she is blessed and appreciative of every aspect of her life. Most assuredly it was painful, but as she became a disciple of the Word of God, she also came to have a relationship with God the Father, Son, and Holy Spirit.

One may ask, "Why should I give my life to a God that made Sister go through so many trials and tribulations as she was trying to be a better person?" Sister's response is, "We all have sinned and have fallen short of the glory of God" (Romans 3:23). As we read about those in the biblical writings, no one was exempt from trials, tribulations, tests, and other things they were subjected to." Even Jesus Christ, who was without sin, became sin to redeem us.

One of Sister's major tests, trials, and tribulations was when she had to take legal action against the employer, she worked for more than sixteen years. This was the job by which she provided for her family, church, community, and others. When Sister was encountering these issues with her employer and being out of work, her mother was diagnosed with breast cancer. For over a year, while addressing this issue with her employer, Sister also drove her mother to all her appointments for testing, surgery, chemotherapy, radiation, doctor's referrals, and so on. She not only provided transportation but was included in all major consultations and follow-up appointments.

Although Sister was able to provide caretakers support for her mother's health issues, for the first time in her adult life, she could not provide financial support and assistance because she was not working. In addition, Sister had to give up her apartment because she could no longer afford the rent. She also had to turn in her leased vehicle because she could no longer afford the payments. She could no longer pay for her mother's life insurance policy, which Sister acquired for her mother before she became ill. It was valued for $30K, and it lapsed when Sister was unable to pay the monthly premiums. While Sister was still not working and was involved in legal action against her employer, her mother passed. Her mother only had a personal life insurance policy valued at $5K.

Sister had to reach out to others in order to give her mother a decent funeral and burial. The Lord also provided a means and a miracle to assist her with the funeral costs and other expenses during and after the devastating period. Throughout these occurrences, Sister said, "The Lord never left me or forsaken me." It was during situations and circumstances of such magnitude that she came to realize many things, such as her true relationship with God and others.

Some of Sister's family members became distant when they no longer received her financial assistance. Some people regarded her as having fallen from the grace of God. Some refused to accept her calls as she sought financial assistance or support. Others said evil and false things about her. Some people did not speak to her for years because they believed she made poor decisions about her life and the church. Those were just some of the forms of rejection and judgment she encountered. And there were many others.

Sister later realized, had she not experienced the trials and tribulations, she most likely would not have come to know the true character of those she believed loved, respected, and appreciated her. After seeing them for who they really were, Sister prayed for them. She sought God's help as she referenced the Words of Jesus Christ: "Father, forgive them, for they know not what they are doing" (Luke 23:34a).

Sister knew that this was what was applicable to her as well. She also knew that she needed the Spirit of God to help her recall this passage of scripture when she remembered her shortcomings and those who subjected her to their evil acts.

During her trials, tribulations the Lord blessed her with help from both male and female Christians who not only heard the Word of God but were disciples who applied the biblical doctrines. They include, many other church members who prayed for her; Christians who took her calls, listened, and attempted to help; Christians who encouraged her while others misjudged her; Christians who gave a shoulder to cry on; and Christians who offered their homes to visit as others would not open a door. Sister also has Spiritual moms who, throughout these occurrences, have prayed for Sister and continue to pray for her. There is a Spiritual mom who could not afford to assist Sister financially but has given her something more valuable as she serves as her godmother, mentor, adviser, listener, and as a gift from God.

Sister has other Spiritual mothers from the churches she once attended, and they are still in contact on a regular basis. She thanks God for every one of them, and they all have special places in her heart.

Sister knows if she did not have those and others who provided Spiritual and financial support, her life would undoubtedly have been in the deepest of despair. They have been supportive of her call to ministry and her life in general.

Sister attributed all these blessings and more to the Triune God. As Sister gave so much of herself and of her possessions, the Lord, our God, blessed her and kept her despite those who rejected her.

To those giving yourselves to God through Christ Jesus, your decision is not in vain. Regardless of what you encounter, "He rewards those who diligently seek Him" (Hebrews 11:6b).

Regardless of all that Sister incurred throughout her life, the LORD sustained her with a life that only He could give, and no one could take away. She quotes the passage of scripture "One thing I do know. I was blind but now I see!" (John 9:25b) She was not physically blind but had an inability to see some of her sins and those of others.

After receiving the Spiritual insight given by God, she realized His love as that stated in the Biblical writings. It is a love of the living God. A love that is everlasting an eternal.

By His mercy and grace through Christ Jesus,

He allowed her to encounter all her situations and experiences and truly worked it all together for her good. When she was in crisis of being overwhelmed with the hardships and her enemies, she had to turn to Him even more to make it through and recover. When there were times of exhaling and seemingly things were not as chaotic, He also had her to depend on Him and be in contact with Him daily.

It was a daily need of prayer and relationship. A relationship that He was not only the true and living God but He was "Abba" her Spiritual Father. A Father who knows His child(ren) and makes the perfect decisions for their well-being. A Father who is patient and loving with His child(ren) when they stray from His upbringing, development, and transformation. A Father who will not force Himself to be accepted as He gives us free will to accept or reject Him.

The more we resist the longer it takes to have that spiritual relationship which is beyond our mere comprehension yet it is worth more than any combined values of the world.

CHAPTER NINE

*Loving God the Father,
Son, and Holy Spirit*

Love the Lord your God with all your
heart and with all your soul and with all
your strength. These commandments
that I give you today are to be on your
hearts. Impress them on your children.
Talk about them when you sit at home and
when you lie down and when you get up.

—Deuteronomy 6:5–7

> Love the Lord your God wit and with all
> your heart and with all your soul and with
> all your mind and with all your strength.
> The second is this: "Love your neighbor
> as yourself. There is no commandment
> greater than these."
>
> —Mark 12:30–31

For a long time, Sister found these two scriptures and other similar scriptures complicated and difficult to understand. She did not understand how anyone is expected to love God with "all your heart, soul, mind, and strength." She considered that as wives are to love their husbands and children, and husbands are to love their wives and children, and if we are extending it to others, then how can we comply with the command to love God with all?

As Sister matured in age and spiritual growth, she developed a deeper love of God. She realized that in all her life's experiences and complications, if she focused on loving God with "all," then she would have had less heartache, confusion, and disappointment by looking for love in the wrong places and people.

To that point, she realized that attempting to love God with "all" will help develop a standard of love that provides the wholesomeness of your spiritual being that extends to Him, yourself, and others as you are loving God. He develops your understanding and life in His love that as you love others spiritually, you are loving Him.

Sister believes her most significant sinful act was not attempting to first love God with "all" of her heart, soul, mind, and strength. Surely, He deserves this from everyone. The major heartache of many in relationships with others is when the other person does not provide the same or more love, respect, and regard. Yet how is it that we do not consider how God feels about the one-sided feelings most have toward Him.

Examples:

- Those who love Him only if He gives them what they want.
- Those who love Him only when He gives you what you think you need.
- Those who love Him only when their lives are pleasant, peaceful, and fulfilled.

- Those who want nothing to do with God when things do not work out the way they think they should.
- Those who are hurt by others and believe God should have intervened, so they blame God.
- Those who lose a love one and blame God.
- Those who experience tragic occurrences and blame God for not protecting them.

In the Bible there are passages regarding a conversation Jesus had with the Sadducees. They asked him a question and His response were as follows:

> Jesus replied, "Are you not in error because you do not know the Scriptures or the power of God?" (Mark 12:24)

Those who turn away from God deny themselves the opportunity to be united with the Most High God, who loves us so much that He gave His only begotten Son. To disallow you and the children to learn, know, and have a relationship with God will result in child(ren) turning to others who cannot provide what only God can and does for His children.

Will we allow the work of the enemy to prevent our children from learning who they are as Christians? Have you considered that if we do not prepare children for Spiritual growth and development, it will eventually affect their lives as adults? Who and what will they turn to when they encounter life's trials and tribulations?

It is believed that sinful acts are more of a reaction or response to sinful acts or situations that an individual experienced as a victim. Consequently, the victim commits harmful acts on others in retaliation. This does not excuse the victim, but it is evident too many people are being secretly victimized and not getting physical, mental, or Spiritual assistance.

Sister realizes that being a Christian does not exclude sinful behavior. She believes that Christians display more sinful behavior as they believe that the only thing required of them is to attend the Sunday church worship services. More unfortunate is that most do not realize they are not aligned or living according to the Word of God. Christianity in the twenty-first century seems more focused on the music provided at Sunday services. It is the music that draws crowds of those seeking to be entertained.

SISTER'S PRAISE

She is thankful to God, His Son and our Savior Jesus Christ, the Holy Spirit, and heavenly hosts for her life and all her trials and tribulations. Through Christ Jesus, God worked it all together for her good (Romans 8:28).

Thankful for everyone, as some loved, supported, and encouraged her, while others subjected her to various forms of cruelty, rejection, hardships, and other evil acts.

SISTER'S PRAISE TO GOD FOR HER DECEASED FAMILY MEMBERS

Thankful for her mother. Despite having limited education, she provided Sister with the wisest decision any parent or person can make for the child(ren) and that is to train them up by sending them to church to learn of and receive the biblical teachings and ministry tools for the Christian life.

Thankful for her stepfather as she believed he had mental health issues that prevented him from being who and what he needed to be as a father and husband. Sister is thankful for the relationships she was able to have with his mother and extended family. Sister as adult was informed her step father and his family actually did not believe she was his biological child.

Thankful for her biological father that while spending thirteen years in prison, he did not deny Sister the opportunity to know the truth about the identity of her father. On his release, he developed a relationship with Sister and his grandchildren. He and his wife provided a family relationship with their five sons, Sister, and their extended family. His wife (Sister's stepmother) provided for their family throughout all the years of her husband's incarceration, visited him with their sons, took Sister to meet her father for the first time, and encouraged her husband when he was released. She was poor but rich in her faith and life in Christ Jesus. Sister is also very thankful for the support that was given by both her father and stepmother in her call and service to the ministry and the proclamation of the gospel.

To all readers of this book, Sister recommends that you also read the following scriptures:

Deuteronomy 6
Isaiah 53
Numbers 23:19
Jeremiah 29:11
Psalm 25: 4-5
John 3:16
2 Timothy 3:16,17
2 Timothy 4:7, 8
2 Corinthians 1:18, 19a, 20, 21
Roman 8:28

IN CLOSING

And those he predestined, he also called; those he called; he also justified; those he justified, he also gloried. He who did not spare His own Son, but gave him up for us all Who will bring any charge against those whom God has chosen? It is God who justifies Who shall separate us from the love of Christ? No, in all these things we are more than conquerors through him who loved us. For I am convinced that neither death nor life, neither angels nor demons, neither the present nor the future, nor any powers, neither height nor depth nor anything else in creation, will be able to separate us from the love of God that is in Christ Jesus our Lord. (Romans 8:30–38)

May the love and Word of God make you whole in Christ Jesus. Amen.

ABOUT THE AUTHOR

The Author is telling a non-fiction story of the life of someone who is commonly referred to as "Sister." It is the story that is revealed in attempts to help others who have and possibly continue to struggle with their past and present life. A life that questions who you really are in contrast with your own identity verses that which are portrayed of you by others.

Sister is someone who has lived a life which many can identify. A life of being confused at times of the things done by your parents, siblings, relatives, friends, enemies, and people in general; life whereby you are not without sin and thankful for the lessons you learned; life that required decisions to be made and it was done to the best of one's ability and circumstances. It is a life of a child who grows up believing it is her responsibility to help others and enjoys doing so. She later encounters those who takes her kindness for weakness and rejects her because her life and purpose is not common to family, society or the church.

She thereafter struggles with who she is and why she is rejected. During this self-analysis God reveals Himself to her in a way that is nothing less than a miracle. She realizes that this God and His love is the answer to everyone's primary need. She unselfishly wants to expose herself by having her story told in efforts to help others who are "searching" for a wholesomeness that provide the vital essentials to a rewarding life.

As one form of love, appreciation and reverence to God the Father, our Savior Jesus Christ, and the Holy Spirit, Sister is donating all proceeds acquired from the sale of this book to be given to a designated church that is renovating to accommodate additional space needed for the children and adult "Bible Study and Sunday School."

Printed in the United States
By Bookmasters